I0126748

Chris Wheeler

Rhymes of the Road and River

Chris Wheeler

Rhymes of the Road and River

ISBN/EAN: 9783744728362

Printed in Europe, USA, Canada, Australia, Japan

Cover: Foto ©Thomas Meinert / pixelio.de

More available books at **www.hansebooks.com**

RHYMES

OF THE

ROAD AND RIVER

By CHRIS. WHEELER

Lays of Lancaster Pike;

Songs of the Schuylkill River;

Bent Oars and Broken Spokes;

Cycling Bab Ballads.

———— ✦ ————

PHILADELPHIA:

E. STANLEY HART & CO.

1885.

TO

My Friend,

EDGAR C. HOWELL, Esq.,

IN REMEMBRANCE

OF

MANY PLEASANT ASSOCIATIONS,

AND AS A SLIGHT TOKEN OF SINCERE ESTEEM,

THIS BOOK

IS INSCRIBED

BY

THE AUTHOR.

PREFACE.

THE author makes no pretensions and therefore tenders no apologies for what the reader may find in this book, even though he is aware of the fact,—unknown perhaps to those of his friends who pressed him to publish this volume,—that he might, and perhaps will, do better if ever he falls into the publishing pit again. With respect to this book, he washes his hands completely of, and makes over to several sanguine and enthusiastic friends, all responsibility attached to the act of issuing from the press what he feels is after all but a gathering together of random rhymes; many of them too hastily and thoughtlessly written, all of them perhaps too carelessly collected, and placed in the hands of a publisher, to receive from him more attention, whether merited or unmerited, than very probably they obtained from the author of their existence.

So Chris tenders no apologies for his " Rhymes." No, not even to the ultra cultured intellects of Boston, though in the neighborhood of the " Hub " are centred some of his earliest recollections, recollections of a time when though oars bent and flashed across Massachusetts waters, no noiseless rubber-hoofed steed carried a rider over the roads of Cape Ann, or bore him to a seat on the rocks of Cohasset.

So much for the general public, in case it should— unfortunately for itself—be brought into any sort of relationship with this book. As for my numerous and kind friends in Philadelphia, amongst whom for four years I have had generously tendered to me and have enjoyed those social relationships and sympathies which sometimes we value too lightly ; I will allow that in this special case, it is but a poor return for me to add to my many faculties for testing their long-suffering good nature, the most questionable one of calling into existence and unloading upon them the " bore " of a book.

                                        CHRIS WHEELER.

WEST PHILADELPHIA, September 20th, 1885.

CONTENTS.

LAYS OF LANCASTER PIKE.

vii.

SONGS OF THE SCHUYLKILL RIVER.

BENT OARS AND BROKEN SPOKES.

CYCLING BAB BALLADS.

LAYS OF LANCASTER PIKE.

TO MY BICYCLE.

MY bicycle! my brave old steed!
   I would not part with 'thee
Were all the pleasures life could give
   Flung in its lap for me;
I would not give the glorious sense
   Of joy bound in thy wheel,
For all the vaunted pleasures life
   Could, or could not reveal.
For where can I so surely find,
   Outside of human kind,
A friend like thee, who never fails
   To ease this tired mind?

I only sought in thee for what
　My other pastimes yield,
But now, I would not give thee up
　For all in pleasure's field.

I love the motion of thy rush,
　The cool air coursing free
Away behind, where vanished scenes
　Have left their smile with me,
The pulse's throb, the panting breath,
　The lazy, lingering stroll,
The leaves of nature's book, which oft
　The old dame will unroll;
All speak to me in varied tones,
　And tell the same old tale,
They sing the same sweet song that breaks
　From wood, and height, and vale—
The same old tale that lives and laughs
　Within the streamlet's flow,
The same old song that's softly sung
　'Mid trees where breezes blow.

They nourish still my dearest wish,
  My wild, untamed desire,
To revel in a life of which
  The heart could never tire ;
'To ramble where, unfettered with
  The tramm'ling laws of men,
I find no mark to bid me shun
  Rude height or rocky glen.
Yes, thou canst bear me swift to where
  In semblance nature still,
Holds sway o'er scenes that once but knew
  And owned no other will
Save that, which bade the river run
  As it had run before,
Save that which threw no steel track down
  Along its level shore.

My brave old " wheel !" my true old " wheel !"
  Thou'lt bear me oft again,
'Mid scenes and sounds that own no rule
  Save that of nature's reign ;

The cares that will beset our life,
  Born of the strife that brings
To hearts and hands the semblance but
  Of fortune's gilded rings,
Are scattered by thy kindly aid,
  Are flung where far behind,
They vex no more the heart that yields
  Its dearest rights to mind.
The showy tribute wrung from life
  By eager, grasping hands,
Is after all but gold foil wrapped
  Round griping iron bands;
The shining gleam, the tempting blaze,
  Of glory lingering there,
Creeps in at last and crushes out
  The life that lives by care.

Then bear me on, my gallant wheel;
  No pulse of life may dwell
Within thy limbs of burnished steel,
  Which serve thy master well;

But still it seems to me that oft
 An answering thrill from thee,
Gives back some free-born fancy, drawn
 By nature's touch from me.
Then bear me on, we leave afar
 The wheel of human strife
And, listening, hear a voice that whispers,
 Cycler, love thy life.

AMERICA'S SONG OF THE "WHEEL."

CYCLING'S summons is sounding far
　　O'er each Commonwealth proud that owns a star,
In the dark blue ground of the banner grand,
That flings its folds o'er our fatherland;
　　And where'er outflung, unfurled, unrolled,
　　That summons leaps from each falling fold.

From the hardy land of the wild north breeze,
Where the pine knots blaze and the great lakes freeze,
To the land where cousins in Southern clime
Have strung a new spoke in the "wheel" of time,
　　Flies the welcome message which makes us feel,
　　What a union link is the steed of steel.

18

And the new spoke fitted in Southern land
Is as firm and true as the " New South's " hand,
Which has butted that spoke with a Union star,
That was tempered well in the lap of war.
What a mighty bond of peace will steal
O'er the land we love, on the brave old "wheel."

From the tide that washes the " Empire State,"
To the wave that rolls through the " Golden Gate,"
From Alaska's wilds to the " crescent moon,"
From the Northland's cape to the South's lagoon,
Flies the wheelman's summons, that near and far,
Makes a union land 'neath a union star.

And that union star o'er the cluster grand,
That in union bound forms the fatherland
Is progress, one hand on the dome above,
The other linked on the earth with love ;
Oh ! the wheel will link in a long bright chain
The stars which divided might shine in vain.

Let this song be sung to the Northern breeze,
Let its whispers fall among orange trees,
Breathing ever soft o'er the cyclers' way
At the breaking forth or the close of day,
    Linking heart to heart, joining hand with hand,
    Let the "wheel" roll on through the fatherland.

A MORNING RIDE.

SPEED thee well, my bicycle, speed thee well, I say,
    Swiftly thou shalt bear me o'er the traveled way,
        Swiftly by the rambling streams,
        Where we watch the yellow gleams
        Of the wavelets leaping bright
        From dark arches into light,
        Seeking, like the ready mind,
        In the darkness light to find.

Speed thee well, my bicycle, bear me on, I say,
Let thy wheel revolving chase thought of care away,
        Every rustling breeze that blows,
        Every breaking beam that glows,

Every form that beauty takes
From Dame Nature when she wakes,
Fairy ferns and forest flowers,
All! my "wheel," all—all are ours.

Then away, my bicycle, while I urge thee on,
Thoughts of other days flash by that have long since
        gone;
Fondly memory backward trends,
And I see and hear old friends,
See them in the shades that play
Through the leafy curtained way,
Hear them in the breeze that makes
Monotones through bushy brakes.

NIGHT LIGHTS.

FAR on the winding road,
   Wavering slow,
What is that flickering,
   Fast flitting glow?
Stars softly showing,
Lights shyly glowing,
Through trees where, blowing,
   Winds whisper low.

Hark! on the soft breathing,
   Half broken breeze,
Tired with blowing through
   Leaf-laden trees,

O'er the woods sleeping,
Music comes creeping,
Voices are keeping
    Time to the breeze.

Out from the sumac shade
    Glide flashing wheels,
Twining through airy spokes
    Melody steals ;
Cyclers are singing,
Wild notes ringing,
Deep voices flinging up
    Music of wheels.

THE BREEZE OF BRYN MAWR.

ONCE as night was closing o'er Bryn Mawr
And far in the western sky,
Farther than where the summits
Of the wild Alleghenies lie,
And beyond where the mighty Ohio
Gives the "Father of Waters" her hand,
The shades of evening had settled
O'er a silent and sleeping land.

Eastward a breeze had been traveling—-
Traveling the live-long day—
Till it found itself blowing through Bryn Mawr,
And there it resolved to stay;

25

For it said, " Though from far I have journeyed,
   O'er city and village and home,
I find not a place like Bryn Mawr,
   Outstretched 'neath the great blue dome."

This it whispered the leafy guardians
   Who watch over Bryn Mawr town
From the heights of the Chester Valley,
   Whose summits their dark shades crown ;
And they bowed their proud heads with pleasure
   When this tribute the West Wind bore
To the charms of the sleeping homesteads
   They were holding their night watch o'er.

And all that was said in whispers
   To the ears of the drowsy trees,
Who stayed for a few short moments
   The way of that Western breeze,
Has been told and retold so often,
   That the fame of this hamlet sweet
Has crept where the wild East breezes
   Wait that Western breeze to greet.

But at Bryn Mawr this breeze has tarried
    Since then, which was long ago—
So long that it seems a wonder
    That it long has not ceased to blow.
'But it dwells near the Chester Valley,
    That it may, when the sun goes down,
Blow a song to the hill of Devon,
    And a whisper through Bryn Mawr town.

A CYCLING YARN TOLD ON LANCASTER PIKE:

C OME, Charlie, wake up, a song for your "wheel"
    As it lies on the grass, while near it
We dozen bold cyclers are lounging at ease,
    And waiting and longing to hear it—
Come, Charlie, wake up, though we haven't a cup
    To drink to your health while you sing it.
"All right," said old Charlie, "I'll sing; but here, Vic,
    Bring your patent new gong out and ring it.

     *   *   *   *   *

There once was a jolly old "wheel," boys,
    And that jolly old "wheel" was mine—
What's the matter with you and your gong, Vic?
    You're the deuce of a fellow for time;

There now, that will do, keep it up so—
　What I'm going to tell you about
Is how I and that precious old "wheel" there
　Came precariously near falling out.

Now here's just the way the thing happened:
　It was only one summer ago
That I got the—well, the marrying fever,
　Which none here have experienced, I know.
And where do you think that I got it?
　Why, down at the seashore, of course,
Where with ducking the girls I'd grown nervous,
　And with whisp'ring at hops I'd grown hoarse.

It was just at the close of the season,
　And friends were all dropping away,
That I struck up an awful flirtation
　With sweet little Miss Jennie Ray.
I tell you I went it in earnest,
　And I thought I was gone, boys, for sure,
In which case I'd have looked like Miss Jennie's
　Blue frock, only fifty times bluer.

Her father was rich as old Crœsus,
    That mighty fine hero of old,
Whose dearest of earth's many pleasures
    Lay in roping in millions of gold;
So old Ray had his millions of dollars,
    In stocks, bonds, and railroads, and cash,
And the man who could wed with Miss Jennie
    Would presumably not be termed rash.

For Jennie was petted and pretty—
    Not proud, though she'd reason to be,
That is, if money's considered,
    For there she was top-o'-the-tree—
That's one thing I must allow of her,
    She certainly never was vain,
Though each dude of "Atlantic" stared at her,
    As he chewed up the end of his cane.

Well, she nodded to Jones on the porch once,
    Who lay half smothered up in his rug,
Then she turned to admire just one other
    Brand new importation—a pug.

Then, turning to me, she said sweetly,
 In tones pitched too highly, I fear,
" I think that the wildest creations
 From England now come over here."

Then said I to myself, " Mr. Charlie,
 Miss Jennie is wondrously fair,
And of sense she possesses a trifle,
 Though her father's a fat millionaire."
And that's how it all came about, boys,
 And we started in earnest at once,
And bicycler Charlie cut out, boys,
 Atlantic's sweet dudes for the nonce.

And we walked and we talked and we flirted,
 Most outrageously, openly bold,
And that wretched dude Jones, with most studied
 Contempt, was left out in the cold ;
And things were all sliding on smoothly,
 Hearts getting quite hot, I could feel,
When the whole blessed business was busted
 By that deucedly unlucky " wheel."

You see, here is how the thing happened :
    I was speeding along one dark night,
After leaving the radiance behind me
    Of Jennie's sweet eyes smiling bright;
And it must have been from the contrast
    Of changing their light for the dark,
That I came in collision with some one
    And ripped up our mutual bark—

Ripped up our bark, you may say so,
    In a double sense, too, you can bet,
For the chap I ran down seemed determined
    To swear himself into a sweat;
And I, you may certainly reckon,
    Felt as riled as himself at the mess,
And since he seemed disposed to talk Latin,
    I, too, felt like talking, I guess.

So a mutual roar of expletives
    Was wafted aloft on the air,
And I was a " d—d public nuisance,"
    And he was a "crusty old bear;"

And I'd be "consigned to old Pluto,"
  And he'd "go to heaven the wrong way,"
When, "great Scott!" a gas lamp shone on him,
  And revealed to me old Johnny Ray.

You just bet I caved, and I mounted,
  And "by George!" you'd have sworn that "old Nick"
Was traveling hard on my hind wheel
  With his toe gathered up for a kick;
For I left the old gent in the roadway,
  Swearing hotly, "You d—d Charlie C——,
Come back;" but I sloped, for I knew, boys,
  'Twas all up between Jennie and me.

So it was, for next morning quite early
  There came such a sweet little note,
Which told me that I and Miss Jennie
  Could never form crew of one boat;
And I tell you I felt for a short while
  As I never once more want to feel,
And I vowed on the spur of the moment
  That I'd wreck that confounded old "wheel."

But I didn't, and there she stands yonder,
    And, boys, my advice to you now
Is, before you join hands with the daughter,
    With the dad have a scriptural row ;
And then, if the girl's worth the having,
    She'll make the old gentleman keel,
And if not, why, your best plan of action
    Is right about face, and then wheel.

A SONG OF LANCASTER PIKE.

O'ER Lancaster's level,
  O'er Lancaster's grade,
Up hill and down hill,
 By coppice and glade,
By woods whence the light
 Of the recreant day,
Long hours ago
 Melted slowly away :

  Cycle, O cycle!
   Come bear me along,
  To where in sweet Bryn Mawr
  A bird sings a song.

35

Let Lancaster's level
  Fall fading behind,
Let Lancaster's grade
  Call no fears to the mind;
By house and by hamlet,
  By village and town,
With a rush we go up,
  But again to rush down.

    So, cycle, my cycle,
      Come bear me along,
    Ere night shadows sadden
    A fair maiden's song.

Old Lancaster's level
  Flies fast to the rear,
Old Lancaster's grade
  Gives us never a care,
While each Lancaster maiden,
  As past her we fly,

Throws a glance of surprise
  At the form flitting by:

    But cycle, O cycle!
    Let the maidens alone,
  For we have in Bryn Mawr
  A sweet maid of our own.

ON THE ROAD.

A WAY we go on our wheels, boys,
   As free as the roving breeze,
And over our pathway steals, boys,
   The music of wind-swept trees;
And round by the woods and over the hill
   Where the ground so gently swells,
From a thousand throats in echoing notes
   The songster melody wells.

Along we speed o'er the road, boys—
   The road that we love so well;
Those oaks know the whir of our wheels, boys,
   And they welcome the cycler's bell ; .

And down in the hollow the streamlet flows
  In rollicking humor along,
While flinging its wavelets' cadence up
  To challenge the cyclers' song.

Above us we feel in the air, boys,
  A spirit that's kin with ours—
A spirit that gives to our life, boys,
  The brightest of earth's best flowers ;
For the health and the strength that are beauty's own,
  That are stamped with nature's seal,
Are securely bound and circled round
  In the spokes of the flying " wheel."

BRYN MAWR TOWN.

O NE night I went a-riding,
    A-riding, a-riding,
Dimly shone the stars where the clouds
Were drifting high ;
And deep among the trees
The trembling summer breeze
Swung the branches into music songs
Which sang good-bye.

By-and-by I came a-riding,
A-riding, a-riding,
Riding down the roadway right into
Bryn Mawr town,

Where welcome gleams of light
Shone from many a window bright;
And stooping in the saddle 'neath
The branches bending down,
I seemed to hear an echo song
Which sang " good-night."

Shortly after I went riding,
A-riding, a-riding,
While a handkerchief flew waving from
A window-casement high;
But the breeze was fast increasing,
And now, blowing without ceasing,
It swept away a gentle song
Which sang "good-bye."

Then I went a-riding,
A-riding, a-riding.
Riding right away from
Pleasant Bryn Mawr town;

Looking back I saw her light
Streaming from the casement height,
And bending where the branches
Brushed my helmet, drooping down,
The whistling wind swept back my song,
" Good-night, good-night."

THE PIKE PUMP.

H ERE once again, our journey completed,
  I and my wheel feel like taking a rest,
Thirty miles ridden and three toll-men cheated,
  That's a record I'll chalk down as one of my best.
"Health to my wheel" I pledge, and I drink it,
  While she stands on her head by yon hickory stump,
Health to a "wheel!" Odd toast you may think it,
  Odder still, as the nectar's derived from a pump.

Odd though it be, I pledge and I mean it,
  And non-cycling readers may laugh as they please,
Perhaps they'd laugh more at my "wheel" had they
   seen it
  As it stood on its head 'neath those hickory trees—

43

Stood on its head, for certain it did, sir,
  After taking an awfully buck-boardy jump,
While I, with the thwack of an auction's last bid, sir,
  Descending, brought mine on the head of the pump.

Thirty miles ridden and three toll-men cheated,
  A machine on its head with its wheels in the air,
A pair of new breeches which must be reseated—
  This last was a thought which impelled me to swear.
A log in the roadway, a dent in the gravel,
  And a head boasting one superfluous bump,
A hole in a cap, and, without doubt or cavil,
  A decided imprint on the head of a pump.

A RIDE AT THE CLOSE OF WINTER.

THUS, thus do I leap to the saddle and fly,
    While the woods wave their arms where the
        spring grasses lie;
E'er enrobing once more in the harmony guise,
In which nature, enveloping, smothers their sighs,
Granting to them instead the soft whispers that fling
Breathings soft as the velvet born leaves of the spring.

Yes! thus once again will my "wheel" bear me on,
Each pedal-push bids some dull trouble begone;
Each turn of the wheel to each draw on the bar
Throws a thrill of delight that will leave lying far
In the distance behind, as in life that's gone by,
What remembering we fain would, forgetting, let die.

45

DEVON, FAIR DEVON.

COME, cycle! we'll wander together away
    As free as the airy pressure
Of the unseen hand that boldly plays
    Through the woodland's leafy treasure.
We'll roam where, far in the western sky,
    There are signs that the veil of even
Has, creeping far from the city's side,
    Dropped down its dark shade o'er Devon.

        O Devon! fair Devon!
        Shadows may close over Devon,
        But there's light in an eye
        That's as deep as the sky
        When it smiles its brightest o'er Devon!

Come, cycle! old Lancaster's arm is outstretched
   To the West, and its trees are bending
Their branches, to shield us from tribute which
   The lowlands unasked are sending.
So forward, on! by each hill and dale,
   For at present our earthly heaven
Lies far away, where the brave old pike
   Takes a turn round the hill of Devon.
      O Devon! fair Devon!
      Dull grows the sky over Devon,
      But there's light in an eye
      That is black as the sky
      On the darkest of nights at Devon.

TIGHTENED SPOKES.

IN my "wheel" there's a spoke that never loosens,
  In the handle a bar that never bends,
And so tried and true are these faithful servants
  That they hold in my heart the place of friends.

There are spokes in the wheel of time that tighten,
  That yield not their hold as the years roll by;
They are mostly thoughts that are linked with the love
  Of the friends who now are no longer nigh.

48

TO J——.

J—— ——, well I know that nothing
I have written here you'll miss;
Therefore, e'er you lift another
Leaf, just waste a thought on Chris.

49

SONGS OF THE SCHUYLKILL RIVER.

BEAUTIFUL SCHUYLKILL.*

BEAUTIFUL Schuylkill,
 Pride of our Park,
River, thou'rt noble still
 As when the bark
Of the red Indian,
 Warrior brave,
Swept its wild master
 Over thy wave.

Beautiful Schuylkill,
 Said he, with pride,
As he swept over
 Thy tree-shaded tide:

* "In Fairmount Park."

" O'er this, my country—
    My fatherland—
Dares the invader
    Stretch his false hand ?"

Beautiful Schuylkill,
    Beautiful still—
Rocky glen, foaming stream,
    Forest, and hill ;
Rivulet, streamlet,
    Steal to thy side,
As to her lover's arms
    Nestles the bride.

Beautiful Schuylkill,
    O'er thee we throw
Shadows that nature
    Never lets grow ;
Yet thy fair features
    Of forest and hill,

All—picture river,
  Are beautiful still.

Beautiful Schuylkill,
  Time steals from thee
Less than it ever
  Can wrestle from me;
Winter and summer,
  Autumn and spring,
O'er thy broad bosom
  Fresh beauties fling.

Beautiful Schuylkill,
  Time will soon steal
One who has loved thee,
  One who could feel
Nature's own hand
  Stretched forth ere she died,
Where man's creations
  Marred thy bright tide.

CYCLING BY THE SCHUYLKILL.

CYCLING in the even'
    When the sun sinks low,
Cycling through the twilight
    While the shadows grow,
Cycling on in starlight
    Underneath the glow,
That falling finds a home
    In Schuylkill's silent flow.

Tell me not that tribute
    From the heart, can find,
Naught to frame in words
    But what, was left behind,

56

By dwellers with and lovers of
　　Old Nature kind,
Whose every virtue by-gone hearts
　　And pens, have lined.

No, tell me not that nothing new
　　Fair Nature gives,
Say not that nothing new
　　In thought, or fancy lives—
Lives not to greet the soul
　　That has, for beauty eyes,
Lives not to furnish yet
　　The fire, that never dies.

AN AUTUMN RIDE UP THE WISSAHICKON.

SEASON of the sun-browned leaf
  Merging into golden hues,
Where the oak and maple meet
  And their leafy harvest fuse;
Shadow-guarded, up the glen,
  See! fair Wissahickon's flow,
Bears away the tribute which
  Oak and maple fling below.

Season of a great farewell,
  Spoken low in accents soft,
Whispered by each leaf that falls
  From the curtain arched aloft;

Stretching o'er us as we ride,
　Oak and maple arches bright,
Sun-browned, merging into gold,
　From our path close out the light.

Timid toned and very soft,
　Lightly tuned and very low,
Soft-breathed songs from sunless streams,
　Trickling where the fern leaves grow,
Greet our ear, and whisper where,
　Hidden by the frondine shade,
Wandering waters seek a home
　Through the path their songs have made.

Gushing, gasping o'er the stones,
　Gurgling round the green-lipped rocks,
Ruder song from rougher streams,
　Surly toned, the quiet mocks—
Surly toned and angry waved,
　White lipped, black browed, bubble crowned,
Wilder streams with wayward will
　Fling their harsher cadence round.

Through the shadow up the glen,
    Where the sunlight's slanting ray
Rarely seeks to share the scene,
    With the rambling breezes play,
Ride we when the evening hour
    Falls o'er Wissahickon's stream,
Losing Schuylkill far behind
    In a sun-browned golden dream.

ON THE SCHUYLKILL.

SCHUYLKILL River,
    From thy quiver
Launch the trembling shafts of light;
Let thy waves fling, flashing upward,
Kisses caught from moonbeams bright;
Noble river,
Gentle river,
How I love thy face at night.

As thus rowing,
O'er thee flowing,
Swift I love to stem thy stream,
How the oars ever onward

Seem to throw, in fancy's dream,
Fairy flashes,
Where their splashes,
Mingle with the moon's soft beam.

Gently flowing,
Nobly glowing,
While yon streak of silver grows,
Narrowed down to where the curving
Banks their shadows interpose ;
Lazy breaking,
Waves half waking,
Backward far our track inclose.

Sleeping never,
Dreaming ever,
Yet not waking fully free,
Thy old waters have a charming
And half mystic claim to be
Ever giving,
And then living
In the thoughts they give to me.

OAR ECHOES.

TOGETHER, lads, steady,
  The swing of the rowlock
Has wakened the ripples
That sleeping lay still;
And the dip of our oars
Has disturbed the clear image
Flung o'er the waters
From Strawberry Hill.

As the spray falls behind us
Fly the fetters that bind us
To the fast fading city
We've left far behind;

There ! our bold strokes have broken
The last lingering token,
That might bind us to where
Life's at best but unkind.

Together, lads, steady,
Let the unity motto
That pilots our fatherland's
Fortunes be ours;
For there's far-reaching wisdom
In the words which are spoken
When the buds of experience
Break forth into flowers.

Through the spray flitting by us,
Through the dusk creeping nigh us,
Through the cloud which yon moon
Has but now silver-lined;
We can read the old story
Which tells how life's glory
Lies in harmonized union
Of body and mind.

Then together, lads, steady,
The breath of the summer
Is dying o'er woods
That are losing their sheen;
As we bend to our work
Let us value the moments,
Which fortune flings kindly
Life's labors between.

For if life is worth living,
'Tis when summer is giving
The fruits of a spring
That can never return;
And the thistledown straying,
Through the wind o'er us playing,
Leaves behind it a lesson
The oldest may learn.

BY THE RIVER.

THE soft wind is pressing
 The breast of the stream,
Where the waves are caressing
 The moon's fickle beam;
As slowly I'm riding
 Where willow shades creep,
Keeping watch over waters
 That wake not from sleep.

As slowly I wander
 On swift noiseless wheel,
Of these haunts I grow fonder
 Through friendship's broad seal;

And footsteps and faces
  Of comrades and friends,
Fancy oftentimes traces
  Where the willow tree bends.

The breeze has ceased blowing,
  From whence did it come?
But the stream is still flowing
  Away to its home;
And I hear the soft whispers
  Of friends vanished long,
In the ripples that singing
  Get lost in their song.

SONG OF THE PENNSYLVANIA BICYCLE CLUB.

G ATHER, Pennsylvania,
    Hark the bugle call,
Hear the dropping echoes
    Round us faintly fall ;
Mounting, speed we onward
    While the shadows dark,
Close in curtained silence
    Over Fairmount Park.

Fairmount's shadows deepen
    As we speed along,
Hark from off the river
    Breaks the boatman's song,

And the mule bells music
 Down the river track,
Draws from many a " Challis "*
 Answering tinkles back.

Starry world above us
 Looking down below,
See you not our starlight
 Glancing back your glow;
Through the spokes reflecting
 Red and green so bright,
See our stars are winking
 Back your watchful light.

Beauty in the night time
 As there is in day,
Softer shines the starlight
 Than the orb of day;
Softer winds seem blowing,
 Softer breezes creep,

* "Challis Stop Bell."

When they find old nature
Nodding off to sleep.

Softly, Pennsylvania,
   Softly ride and slow,
Noiseless as the mid-stream
   Of yon waters flow;
Now move fast, and faster,
   Yet our swift steeds make,
Sounds less than the ripples
   On those banks that break.

Faster, Pennsylvania,
   Let the bugles ring,
While the echoing hillsides
   Back the wild notes fling.
River song and ripple
   Greet us as we glide,
Near where stars are dipping
   Deep in Schuylkill's tide.

THE LAST SONG.

J—— ——, though old Schuylkill's praises,
    Roughly chanted thus by Chris
You'll forget, yet still the singer's
    Mem'ry you will not dismiss.

BENT OARS AND BROKEN SPOKES,

BENT AND BROKEN ON BOTH SIDES OF THE ATLANTIC.

BENT OARS AND BROKEN SPOKES.

BENT oars and broken spokes,
   How often have I seen them,
How often found a lesson of
   Our life bent in between them;
The rose between two thorns will grow,
   Will even learn to love them,
The lesson learned from broken hopes
   Will raise us oft above them.

Bent oars and broken spokes,
   We lay them down with sorrow,
And seek in something fresh to find
   What we can beg or borrow;

We beg the health we cannot buy
From every breeze that, blowing,
Renerves the friction Time's old hand
Is never tired of slowing.

Bent oars and broken spokes,
Who wants of them to borrow—
Who looks for that which lies but where
To-morrow meets to-morrow.
We seek to find in memory's arms
Friends once our best and dearest,
While greeting still the haze that time
Throws round what once was nearest.

Bent oars and broken spokes,
Of thought and word and action,
Each twisted thread that twines through life
Must lose its last attraction.
The oar that's bent, the twisted spoke,
The nature warped or broken,
Each flung along life's shore lies there,
Of life a rusted token.

A SHADOW HOPE.

IN the clasp of the hand that is clinging in silence,
  In the light of the eye that is lost ere its lash,
Like the lightning's cloud curtain creeps over the heaven
  From whose bosom 'twould seem the bright energies
    flash ;
Dwells assurance which bids me hope on though the
    hoping,
  May live like the cloud that is fated to be,
Swept afar from its friends by that fate which the future
  May fling round this heart that feels love but for thee.
Yes, that clasp tells me more than the thought flashes
    leaping,
  From the eye that reluctant is forced to reveal.

The slumbering power of the passion that proves how
  The heart fails to hold all it ever can feel ;
I dare not say more, I shall never, can never,
  Feel love for another that as equal with thee,
Will live on in this heart which though never forgetting
  The past, will forgive you what yet has to be.

———

ROLL on, my Cycle! Life is what
  Its children choose to make it ;
And pleasure comes to all alike
  Who reach a hand to take it.

SOUVENIR.

CYCLE! Cycle! trusty Cycle!
   How I dearly love thee,
Flashing, glancing out as bright
   As any star above me;
Far away, and farther, farther,
   You will bear me fast,
Till receding Boston's turmoil
   Dies away at last.

Cycle! Cycle! my own Cycle!
   You and I are flying
Faster than those city echoes
   Far behind us dying;

Then away and over hillside,
  Climbing like a feather,
Or, as lightning rushing downward,
  Ride we on together.

Cycle! Cycle! we have wandered
  Many a mile together,
We have tasted summer sunshine,
  Storm and winter weather,
And I think as through the starlight
  Slowly now we glide,
Through our spokes north winds have whistled,
  Western winds have sighed,
Now where Boston's breeze is blowing,
  England's breezes died.

A RIVER DREAM.

LET the oar rest ere again it revels
 In the breast of the stream that in darkness lies,
A type of the thought that remains unspoken
 In the liquid depths of that sweet girl's eyes;
Her hand droops down where the wavelet's ripple
 Creeps up to caress what I fain would hold,
But I never can, for the wave's soft lapping
 Scarce hides on one finger a band of gold.

Let the oar strike on the sleeping water,
 Let the eyelash cover the tell-tale light,
Which I feel creeps up with unbidden fervor
 From a fire that burns with a flame too bright;
Let the oar bend, let the thought bend with it,
 Let it, bending, break through that passing wave;
Let the thought break through a brief dream that dying,
 Can forever keep what it never gave.

FRIENDSHIP'S INFLUENCE.

TELL me what tributes of friendship
Are cherished the closest by you,
Tell me what virtues stand highest
In thine eyes, be they many or few;
For be they as many and royal
As man ever held or can hold,
It shall be my life's labor to win them,
They shall be to me silver and gold.

Knowledge may kneel to the simple,
May seek him while being unsought,
Honor may come to the careless,
Both may in a measure be bought;
But virtue asks never a master,
Though vice may seek many a slave,
Yet she answers when called, as the bravest
May often be led by the brave.

"GOOD-BYE, ROB."

A LAY OF A LONDON HOSPITAL.

I MISS them, Rob, I miss them,
  Those fields of sunny green;
The two soft, mossy, shelving banks
  And the running stream between;
I see no more the wind-wave sweep
  Across the fields of grain,
And the summer breeze 'mid summer trees,
  I will never hear again.

I see them not, I hear them not,
  Those old time friends of mine,
Who sang to me, as I to them,
  Full oft and many a time;

For, went I fast, or went I far,
  On horseback, foot, or "wheel,"
The cadence fresh from feathered throats
  Would o'er my pathway steal.

I see no more the springing flowers,
  Which I have marked so oft,
Wake to new life, when summer blew
  Her whispering breezes soft;
I hear no more, through whirling spokes,
  Those soft winds swiftly play;
Far as they now are from me, soon
  They'll farther be away.

Reach me your hand, old friend, and let
  Me say good-bye once more;
I'm riding now, it seems to me,
  Along a misty shore;
It's growing narrow, shelving down;
  Rob! bring your lantern near,
Rob—say, Rob—when you ride this road,
  Keep your flame burning clear.

It's very dark, yes! and it's cold,
   It's growing cold I feel;
I seem to grasp these handles hard,
   They hold like frozen steel.
' Ha! Rob, old man, I see the light,
   It's burning bright and clear;
Your hand, old friend, we'll meet again
   On a better road than's here.

I CANNOT FORGET.

YOU tell me the day and the hour has gone by
When that hand and that heart could convey one
reply,
To the story of love from a heart like to thine,
Which you say never was and can never be mine.
Yet I say, though I cannot, can never tell why,
Life lives but for me in a glance from thine eye.

The heart that has known what the lips fail to tell
Can never while mem'ry remains say farewell,
The hand that has labored to gain and then lost
Its reward, may forget what that labor once cost,
But remembrance of that which was loved will live
on
In the face of the fate which forbade its being won.

86

MEMORIES.

WHEN my "wheel's" at rest and my oar is sleeping,
     The measured pause of the pulse will tell,
That the minute strokes of thought are turning
     The windlass handle o'er memory's well.

And the lever turns with a slow, slow motion,
     And deep through the gloom the chain drops down;
And the hand grows tired, and the heart grows weary
     Ere the kiss of the waters its mission crown.

Or it turns and turns, as the grasp of the guiding,
     Controlling hand that at first laid hold
Is removed, till the rush of the falling vessel
     Is checked by the clasp of the waters cold.

87

And whether I turn with a slow, slow motion,
  Or whether I let the thought links run
As they will, I still hear the same old cadence
  Come stealing up when the goal is won.

And the refrain sang by the chain links chafing
  And fretting sore, o'er their roller bed,
Brings home to my heart a harvest gleaning
  Of joy and sorrow which I thought lay dead.

AIR WHEELS.

SOFT and still, valley and hill,
  Melt in the evening shadow,
Away behind the western wind
  Creeps across the meadow;
We'll leave it far behind, boys,
  The roads are smooth and fair,
O'er hill and hollow the breeze may follow,
  Follow, follow—air.

Far away, breaking its way
  Out from its tunnel quiver,
The railroad steed with arrowy speed
  Sweeps by the quiet river;

It leaves us far behind, boys,
　　We straggle away in the rear,
Let it go! let it go! to beat it, you know,
　　Our steeds should be made of—air.

Loud then soft, struggling aloft,
　　Over the trees and bushes,
The silver notes of the bugle float
　　Then fall among river rushes;
That means we're near our goal, boys,
　　And friends are waiting there,
Press hard on your wheel, how the wind and the
　　　　steel
　　Make a rushing of air through air.

ONCE AGAIN.

ROUSE thee, my " wheel!" for the winter has wended
Its way to the bourne whence no traveler returns;
The first breeze of spring with its last breeze has blended,
And sung the " Amen " which each season it learns.

Rouse thee, my " wheel!" for the sunlight has beckoned,
From where the red orb rises over yon hill;
Rising earlier still as each morning re-wakens
Its watch which through winter woke cloudy and still.

Rouse thee, my " wheel!" for the notes of the song birds
Come wafted across from the fresh budding trees,
And the swell of their cadence makes melody snatches
Of music, which even friend Orpheus might please.

Rouse thee, my " wheel!" for the hues that have mantled
The light lying clouds of the morning must find
In the cheek of thy master tints such as shall rival
The flush on their own which the sun god has lined.

TO ANNIE ———.

SITTING idly in your chair,
Sitting idly fretting,
Lost to friendship's fond rebuke,
Life and love forgetting ;
Annie, tell me why so sad
When all else on earth is glad.

Can the path of life be rough
To so fair a creature,
Can the world to thee be aught
But a gentle teacher?
Annie, dearest, tell me why
Sadness should not pass thee by.

Living in the lap of ease,
  Friends flung freely round thee,
Sorrow's hand should surely be
  Withered e'er it found thee;
    Why does sadness dwell with thee
    Let it choose its friend in me.

Then the case is as I thought,
  This is then the reason,
This is why thy face so fair
  To thy heart plays treason;
    Fairest face will soonest show
    What sleeps in the heart below.

Years ago I told thee how
  Brave hearts would be broken,
By your words which oft had been
  Better left unspoken;
    Hearts were given men to be
    More than playthings meant for thee.

Yes! I thought so!—now at last!
—And you really loved him,
Idle words in cruel jest
　　Now have far removed him;
　　　Annie, dearest, bear in mind
　　　Life is love, and love is kind.

TOM MOORE'S COTTAGE.

AT THE "MEETING OF THE WATERS," IRELAND.

THROUGH the depth of the valley the sunlight
    Was streaming in lingering love,
As if loath to be leaving a landscape
    That must have dropped down from above;
A landscape where lost in day dreaming,
    All nature seems eager to pour
In the rightly tuned ear of the stranger
    The song which she sang to Tom Moore.

We flung our machines 'neath the shadow
    Of the lord of the forest who hung
Its far-reaching form o'er the cottage
    Where the choicest of songs once were sung;

95

And we wondered what stories its branches
Could tell if they only knew how,
—Then we gazed on the quaint old-time cottage
And thought on the then and the now.

And we hung o'er the rock-fettered water,
And we harked to the sighing of wind
Through the giant-like limbs of the elms
Which the close-clinging ivy entwined;
And we gazed on the waves that had wakened
The silver-tuned lyre of Tom Moore.
Where for us they were meeting and mingling
As they met for the minstrel of yore.

NIAGARA.

A MEMORY OF THE L. A. W. MEET, 1885.

NIAGARA! Niagara!
  The voice of thy waters
Hoarsely confiding their story to me;
Here as I ride round
The shore of this island
  Echoes thy voice like a song from the sea,
Years, many years, have rolled by since I listened
  To that cadence recalled by the song sung by thee.

Oft have I ridden when breakers were rolling
  High o'er the rocks that with iron band
Circle the shore of the country where fortune
  Flung me afar from my own western land.

97

Niagara! Niagara!
I have dreamed that I heard thee,
 In dreams have I gazed on thy wild rushing leap.
In dreams have I wondered if while I was absent
 The thunder riven song of thy waters would sleep.

And now I have heard thee,
Have heard thee and seen thee:
 I have listened in silence as slowly I rode
O'er the pilgrimage pathway that winds round this
 island
 By which through the ages thy eddies have flowed.
I have waited and watched for the moment when
 voicing
 The hope of long years and the dream of a life,
I should look on the rush and the roar of thy rapids,
 And list to the song of thy rock fretted strife.

TWO SONGSTERS OF TWO LANDS.

SINGER sweet of many songs,
  Whose unwritten sweetness
Gives to thee our song-land realm
  In its full completeness;
Pen or pencil fail to tell
  All thy tuneful graces,
Yet, there's one sweet song which yields
  Not to thine embraces.

Singer sweet of England's shore,
  Whose delight is flinging
Wild notes to the night that lives,
  But to hear thy singing;
Singer sweet, thy song to me
  Soars beyond each measure,
Which our mocker flings so free
  At his fickle pleasure.

SONG OF ITALIAN SAILOR ON BOARD THE GUIDO, 1879.

HO! for the blue Tyrhennian Sea,
    Ho! for my own sweet Italy,
Man the crew by the capstan bar,
Furl the sail on each trembling spar,
Hark to the strain that breaks afar,
    Music of Italy.

Sweet as the song that breathes of heaven,
Singing of love on the air of even,
Light as the foam and soft as the sigh
Of the waves on thy shore, O Italy!

Then man the crew by the capstan bar,
Furl the sail on each trembling spar,
Hark to the strain that breaks afar,
    Music of Italy.

Music of music the wide world o'er,
Greets my ear from my native shore,
Stealing aloft to the dreamy sky,
That smiles o'er my own sweet Italy.
Then man the crew by the capstan bar,
Furl the sail on each trembling spar,
Wake! wake! again, my old guitar
    To music of Italy.

MEMORY ARCHES.

I BELIEVE it is true, I have heard it said often
   That love cannot live when it once has grown cold;
And that life worth the living coins memory arches,
   Whose keystones are thoughts which can never be
   told.

I've heard thee say often, should the world presume
   coldly
To trample on feelings it never could know;
That the knowledge would cheer thee that the truth
   could be only
Revealed to this heart whence like sentiments flow.

102

The world will grow older, the world will grow wiser,
   It will widen, and broaden, and burst its old bands;
It will sweep from their niches and will never restore
     them,
   Works which once were the triumphs of hearts and
     of hands.

But deep in their dwelling, which far back through the
     ages,
   And on through the arch of eternity's span;
Were ever—will ever be the thoughts which unspoken,
   Yet fashion the life worth the living by man.

SING ME A SONG.

THE night to the morning
Once sullenly said,
" Why risest so soon
From thy orient bed;
Cannot I with the wealth
Of a star lighted sky,
Give to earth all the light
That owes life to thine eye?"

Said the morn to the night,
" Farewell, my dark maid,
The earth has been loved
Long enough by thy shade;

The love of a night
  May be lost in a day,
But the love born of light
  Will live on for alway."

The tenderest tribute
  The heart can e'er give,
If we wish that it blossom,
  And blossoming live,
Must bear not alone
  Look of star searching eye,
But must stand the bright test
  Of the sun lighted sky.

TO HELEN ——.

A ND she is dead
Whom I remember,
Kind were her words
As her heart was tender;
Loving as light
Which distinction knows not,
Sweet as the flower
That the florist sows not.

Tell it again,
For I now may never
Look on the face
That has left forever

Haunts that were happy
   When hearts beat lightest,
Scenes whose soft beauty
   On her smiled brightest.

That is enough,
   Braving all danger,
In a strange land
   Dying a stranger.
Lady, thy lot
   Was a strong man's measure,
Earth loses what
   Heaven gains—a treasure.

QUERY.

HEART of woman, head of man,
  Read them right who will and can;
Life-long study to the wise,
Half of which the cynic flies,
Which can win and which can wear?
Gems which each should guard with care.

Which can win and which can wear?
Which can from the other tear?
All that's cast in beauty's mold,
All that lives and dies for gold,
Head hurls with unerring hand,
Darts, the heart cannot withstand.

Heart of woman, head of man,
Covers which the widest span?
Captures which the surest prize?
Watchest which with subtlest eyes?
Hearts will break, where heads will bend,
Live man's hopes, where woman's end.

————————

WRITTEN ON THE BACK OF A BIRTHDAY CARD.

SEE the wash of the waters that roll o'er our life
    Sweep over one barrier more,
One rock in the rampart now yields mid the strife
    Cut deep in the next on the shore.

TRIFLES.

HIS was a faded blossom,
Dropping its soft slight head,
Close to a pale leaf lying
Over some petals dead.

Hers was a memory blossom,
Blooming again once more;
Born of a wave of music
Blowing along the shore.

His was a fair face smiling
Over the flower again ;
Hers was a deep voice singing
Words of a magic strain.

But soon the fading flower
　Lay with the lifeless leaf,
And the memory wave of music
　In a sea wave lost its grief.

———　——

THERE'S a steed whose hoofs require no care
　　From the worker 'neath spreading chestnut trees,
There's a ship that safer its freight will bear
　Than the famous sailor of silent seas;
There's a bird that soars through the trembling air
　With surer flight than the one that flees
From the hawk's fell swoop, and the 'cycle fair
　Has coaxed from my pen such lines as these.

THE BROKEN AXLE.

NO light can enlighten
    The heart that is broken,
No hope can re-waken
    The soul that is dead ;
And the lips do not speak
    Words that by the looks spoken
Reveal all and more
    Than can ever be said.

There's light on the hillside,
    And shade in the valley,
There's a smile in the river
    As there's death if you choose ;
So there's light on the forehead
    Though the heart holds a shadow
Which though mourning, it still
    Will reluctlantly lose.

MY FRIEND'S BABY.

BABY Leoni, so curly and coaxing,
  The light of thine eye and the lisp of thy tongue
Have led me to think of the moments when like thee
  I recked not of blessings born but for the young.
    But, Leoni, my darling, the time's creeping on
    When that light will be dimmed, and that lisp will
      be gone.

May the heav'n that smiles on thee now at thy waking,
  Cast round thee the guardianship folds of a love,
Which a tear from thine eye, or a sigh from thy bosom,
  Would demand from the eyes we trust watch from
    above.
    O Leoni, Leoni, may life for thee find
    Not a sorrow to leave e'en a shadow behind.

TO ———.

TELL me not of them,
    The days are gone by,
When glances fell soft
    From thy dark shaded eye;
That day has departed
    When fate could not find
On thy forehead a frown
    That in earnest was lined.

Tell me not of them,
    The words which you said,
Their music soon melted
    Into echoes now dead;

And never, O never
 Can sympathy steal
One sigh for the sorrow
 Which you dare not reveal.

Tell me not of them,
 The songs which you sang,
I shall spurn the last tones
 From my heart where they hang
Like the last leaves of autumn,
 Which lingering cling,
To the branch that forgetting,
 Hopes not for the spring.

WESTWARD, HO!

THE red sun is sinking and flinging to me
   Strange shadows from over the storm-beaten sea,
As the last gleams of light strike the swaying cross-tree,
   Whence I gaze on the wild scud flying.

Behind us the shadows creep after our bark,
The daylight of Eastern skies dies into dark,
There! a wave of wind-music comes sweeping, and hark!
   It sets our slack cordage sighing.

The red sun has sunk out of sight, and the spray
Dashes wild o'er our bows as we drive on our way,
Striving madly it seems—as we strive—day by day,
   To capture the sunlight dying.

AN AFTERNOON RIDE.

THE swallows are sweeping o'er meadow and lea,
   The woodpecker's bill shakes a song from the tree,
There's a breeze on the land blowing in from the sea
      And I and my wheel are flying.

There's a gleam on the waters a sail flashing white,
There's a wash on the rocks and a sparkling of light,
And the foam flakes are falling in crystalline flight,
      Where I and my wheel are lying.

The foam flakes are flying away behind,
The swallows are circling against the wind,
There's a glow on the clouds where crimson lined
      They smother the sunlight dying.

ADIEU.

I ASK for you the brightest smiles
 That life and love can give ;
I ask from you but one small word
 To bid one memory live ;
I cannot tell thee e'er in words
 The mem'ries lying deep
Within this heart, which, true till death,
 Will one dear secret keep.

Heart beats to heart, and life to life.
 O that the frenzied dream,
Which mocked us both, by act or word
 Or thought, I could redeem ;
I cannot, perhaps I dare not hope
 That fate will yet retwine,
Beyond death's stream the one bright strand
 That links this life with thine.

FRIENDSHIP.

WHEN memory steals upon fancy
  And claims, like a dear old friend,
That the past with its lights and its shadows
  With the future should sometimes blend,
Then at moments like these when gazing
  With fancy on some fair scene
I'll turn to my old friend memory
  And think upon what has been.

And if in those years gone over,
  And through the long years to come,
—The past that still speaks so sweetly
  —The future that yet is dumb:
At the end, if I find I have touched not
  A few of the silver keys
Of friendship, my years have passed over
  As shadows o'er sunlit seas.

119

RECREATION.

SOFT whispering word to weary hearts addrest,
How sweet thy music can those hearts attest,
How blest the prospect, how endeared the hour
Which welcomes thee of toil the brightest flower,
When the worn heart and weary mind once more
Seek in thy flowing stream a bounteous store
Of the bright thoughts they cherish, hopes they feel,
And which thy presence can alone reveal.
Can startle from the daily toil and strife
The heart that beats, the soul that gilds the life,
Which in the weary breast would drooping lie
By the stern will of labor doomed to die.
But thy bright cheering presence once again
Renews the drooping spirit, soothes the pain,

Wafts us fresh life, sustains the weary soul,
And from a remnant recreates a whole.
Brightest of earth's best flowers that come to me,
At times, when though the world has grown to be
Less than it ever seemed to be before,
Yet still not paled enough to close the door
Of pleasure quite—comes thy soft touch, and gentle way
Of changing cares to joy, as droops the day
Into the arms of even', with lightest touch
Slanting its shadows, while we marvel much
That the dark curtains though they herald rest
We welcome not, as nature's great bequest.
Brightest of toil's few children, formed to be,
Though last born, laden with best fruit for me.

GIVE ME ALL ——.

L IFE cannot,
   Give ever,
All that
   The heart will crave;
Love cannot,
   Hold ever,
Half what
   It owes the grave;
E'en though that
   Half slumber,
Deep, in
   A memory wave.

BY THE STREAM.

TELL me truly
      While we ride,
   Close this babbling stream beside,
If the words you speak to me
Are not merely meant to be
Little more than bubbles breaking
Knowing naught of constancy;
Little more than loose leaves shaking
At the straying breeze that free,
Whispers low to every tree.

So! you're silent; then I see
Just how much you value me.

123

YOUR AUTOGRAPH, PLEASE.

FRIENDSHIP'S chain fate often fashions
In the lap of chance and flings
Lights and shadows of life's passions
Into all its golden rings.
And perhaps this thought here written,
In some far-off future time
Will recall the eve its author
Roughly threw it into rhyme.

OAR BEND THE LAST.

J—— —— spokes and oars are bending,
   Dust is flying, bubbles hiss,
O'er the stream of life that hurries
   You along as well as Chris;
Therefore, dear, I will allow, that
   In some things I've been remiss.

CYCLING BAB BALLADS.

A LAY OF A RACE.

A RACE for a ribbon a race for a bow,—
Five men are in line, and away they go.
Now, while they go rushing and tearing along,
With the flashing spokes singing the racers' loved song,
Just listen, I'll tell you the reason, old son,
Why a blue ribbon beckons those bold riders on.

You see that brown jersey right there by the tent,
'Neath that white ostrich feather so gracefully bent,
That's Annie, the queen of the day,—
See! she's shaking the ribbon this way.
You know her? you lucky old "son of a gun!"
She's the jolliest girl, and I for one
Will swear she's the handsomest—Robinson does—under
    the sun,
    And she's to present the blue ribbon.

129

The ribbon you see is our annual prize :
One mile is the distance—how Robinson flies !
 And the winner receives the ribbon, you know,
 From the queen of the day, whom you also must know
Is the prettiest girl in town ;
 At least on the present occasion she is—
Ha! there's Robinson in, and the ribbon is his,
See ! Annie is bending down ;
 She pins the ribbon—" by George " she is
A queen, though she wears no crown.

FORTUNE'S like the bicycle,
 She sometimes throws her rider,
And laughing asks him why on earth
 So trustfully he tried her ;
Then winking, laughs again to hear
 Him say, no more he'll ride her.

LANCASTER PIKE.

(The only good road at the time of writing in the vicinity of Philadelphia.)

OH ! of every conceivable road for a bike
    Outstretched anywhere in creation,
Not one of the lot can beat Lancaster Pike,
    In fact, or imagination ;
Folks not in the secret may wonder at this,
    But I tell you it's true to the letter,
When it's good, why it's ever the essence of grand,
    When it's bad, why there's nothing that's better.

Oh ! of every conceivable road for a trike
    That you've known of or read of in story,
Not one can compare with old Lancaster Pike,
    It stands quite alone in its glory.

We have hundreds of miles of most beautiful streets,
    Paved with rocks, but that's nothing to speak of,
For the boys are all right, while we give 'em the " Pike,"
    Which there's only a twenty mile streak of.

Oh ! I've already said we have hundreds of miles
    Of streets, which the world cannot equal,
But the dickens a one can compare with the " Pike,"
    As you'll say when I tell you the sequel.
For of every conceivable road for a ride,
    In this great and most civilized city,
Not one can compare with the Pike, for you see
    There's no other, and so ends this ditty.

A FIRST RIDE.

TIMOTHY JACKSON'S a friend of mine,
  A fellow that's hard to beat,
He's catcher, and pitcher, and bat of his nine,
And he rows like a steamboat that's running on time,
  And to see him eat cream is a treat.

But there's one thing that Timothy tried in vain,
  And that was to mount a machine,
Or rather he mounted, and then it was plain
That Tim had a lightness of head or of brain,
And his wife most certainly thought him insane,
  He raised such a deuce of a scene.

133

The first thing he did when he got on the back
Of his bicycle steed was to holler out "Jack!"
" Jack, you scoundrel! Jack, you dog,
You said it was easy as riding a frog,
Or sitting astride of a rainbow at noon,
And sliding along to the lap of the moon,
Hallo! you scamp, I'm running away,
And there on the hill is a wagon of hay,
Heaven send help, here's the devil to pay."
" Twist to the right," shouted Jack from behind,
And Tim not only twisted but twined,
In an elegant fashion which called to one's mind
The mazy curves and wavy flow
Of the thread Ariadne gave to her beau.

But there's never a lane without a turn,
And there's never a fire but's bound to burn,
There's never a buckle without a bend,
And there's never a story without an end.
And so said Tim when he went for the door
  Of a cottage neat and trim,

And laid it flat on the clean-swept floor
In the midst of a thunderation roar
Of babies and women and children and men,
Who reckoned "old Nick" had broken his pen
And came for his supper on earth, and then,
  To have 'em to supper with him.

Having busted the door the bicycle bent
Its backbone under the table, and sent
  The crockery on an excursion.
And Tim was sitting on cranberry pie,
With a chow-chow pickle patch over his eye,
And he reached for a prayer book and then with a
    sigh,
  Led the family prayer for conversion.

THE LAY OF A RECREANT.

RIDING on a bicycle may all be very nice,
Riding on a tricycle may pay for once or twice,
Riding on a steamboat is purely simply sweet,
But for quiet calm enjoyment buggy riding can't be beat.

Riding in a buggy, boys, behind a trotting mare,
What means of locomotion with a buggy can compare.

Riding on a bicycle you're not allowed a whip,
And except you're on a " sociable " you cannot use your
lip,
Then riding on a steamboat there's a crowd on every
hand,
While you needn't have but two within a buggy on the
land.

136

Riding in a buggy, boys, behind a trotting mare,
What means of locomotion with a buggy can compare.

Riding on a bicycle's a sort of Jersey treat,
A " sociable " is better, for *she* may be very " sweet;"
True, a shady nook or corner on a steamboat you may find,
But there's nothing like a buggy when no bicycler's behind.

Two within a buggy, boys, behind a trotting mare,
The devil take the bicycle that can with that compare.

"LE MISANTHROPE."

NOW do I ride a bicycle,
　　Why, yes, you just can bet
Your bottom dollar that I do
　　And so should you, but yet!
Before you choose your mount, my man,
　　Just look around and try
What bicycle of all on earth
　　Is the worst machine to buy.

For by the luck that prompts a man
　　To buy the crack machine,
I swear that he who buys the best
　　Is most serenely "green;"

Because you know, or if you don't,
　You shortly soon will see,
That about what's good—or worse—what's best,
　Two cyclers can't agree.

It mollifies a fellow quite,
　To tell him he's a fool,
Or to hint quite sweet and gently
　That he'd better go to school;
But the most consoling news when he
　Has bought a new machine,
Is to tell him there's some better mount
　He surely should have seen.

I've had a " Standard," " Special Club,"
　A " Challenge," " Expert," " Star,"
But every time I bought a mount
　Some cycling sage would mar
The satisfaction to be gained,—
　From singling from the rest,
The premier mount—by telling me
　I'd bought the second best.

At present I'm possessor of
  A blooming " Victor Trike,"
For which I changed my " Expert,"
  Which I'd really learned to like ;
And now there's Harry White must owe
  Me some eternal grudge,
For he says I'm such a jackass,
  In not trading for a Rudge.

Now by the hopes that once I had
  Of unity of thought,
About the best I tell you buy
  The worst that can be bought;
For that's the only way to G
  With all your cycling kind,
And the universal verdict will
  Agree with yours you'll find.

THE BRITISHER'S LAMENT

AFTER BUYING AND TRYING TO RIDE AN "AMERICAN
STAR" BICYCLE.

O BROTHERS, listen to the song
    That I'm about to sing,
I tell you that you've never yet
    Experienced such a thing
As I'm about to tell you of,
    Though you've ridden fast and far,
For you've never straddled yet, my friends,
    A d—— Yankee " Star."

And what is that I hear you say,
    In genuine surprise,
Well then, my friends, it's nothing more
    Than what it's name implies ;

Or rather, it's a comet, for,
   Ride you near or ride you far,
The big wheel follows after
   In that d—— Yankee " Star."

You must know I'm not a champion
   Of swearing, as a rule,
And I don't approve of telling tales
   Within, or out of school;
But by every blazing ember
   That burns in heaven afar,
If you want to break your neck, just ride
   A d—— Yankee " Star."

It is a safety bicycle
   Beyond a living doubt,
If safety lies in stomach pumps,
   And turning inside out;
And that is why the doctors all,
   In loving friendship, are
Beseeching you to mount and ride
   A d—— Yankee " Star."

Yes a header's sometimes pleasant
   And often is immense,
When your handles gently hold you back
   From bolting through a fence;
But the pleasure's always lacking
   When a twelve-inch handle bar
Digs you squarely in the stomach
   On that d—— Yankee " Star."

Now that's the fix that I was in
   A few short nights ago,
When horn and steel both strove to get
   Where softer victuals go;
Not only that, my feelings too,
   Which sweetly touchy are,
Were mortified extremely
   By that d—— Yankee " Star."

For Mary saw me coming down
   The street on that machine,
A putting on an awful spurt
   To show I wasn't green;

When just as I was passing by
    Old Tompkins' toy bazaar,
I showed her how I managed that 'ere
    D—— old Yankee " Star."

I've traveled on a stage coach, once,
    And soared in a balloon,
I'd serious thoughts of taking once
    Verne's railroad to the moon ;
I've squirmed upon a camel,
    And an Irish jaunting car,
But devil a one of them all can beat
    That d—— Yankee " Star."

THE BRITISHER'S LAMENT, No. II.

O BRETHREN of the wheel, I'll sing
    You yet another song,
I do assure you that it will
    Be neither short nor long ;
For my wits are fairly flummuxed
    And scattered near and far,
By the anti-human antics
    Of that d—— Yankee "Star."

I seriously had thoughts of steering
    Eastward my canoe,
For I'll tell you what's a secret now
    To all but me and you ;

Since the day I dined on sawdust,
   Near Tomkins' toy bazaar,
Why Mary's cut me just as I
   Cut that d—— Yankee " Star."

She cut me dead, I do declare,
   For what I do not know,
Except for having made myself
   A *handlebar-numbed* show ;
Or perhaps because I cut myself,
   For this confounded scar
Is a legacy bequeathed me by
   That d—— Yankee " Star."

And now there comes to cap my woes
   The story swooping down,
That the "Star," at Philadelphia
   Nearly grabbed the racing crown ;
After hopping round at Springfield
   In a way that dashed afar
My hopes of how grim fate would treat
   That d—— Yankee " Star."

Cycling Bab Ballads.

Not satisfied with having made
   Me court a " Gibson " keg,
For physic kept it's busted now
   Another fellow's leg ;
And I'm told that Hendee 'll have to hire
   A Pullman palace car
To pull the man along who rides
   A d—— Yankee "Star."

And next the pesky thing will shoot
   Across Atlantic's wave,
And influence some noted " cracks "
   To court an early grave;
O darn it all, as Shakespeare says,
   It's going quite too far,
When legs and records both get smashed
   By that d—— Yankee " Star."

I'm going straight to Westminster,
   The " grand old man"* shall hear

* William Ewart Gladstone.

What liberal views have done for wheels,
  You bet he'll quake with fear;
And he'll call a cabinet council,
  And he'll publish near and far,
How the country's going to bust upon
  A d—— Yankee "Star."

DEVON HILL.

IF cycling joys are found among
    Those promised us in heaven,
Let's pray we'll find not one that's like
  That precious hill of Devon ;
"A thing of beauty," says the bard,
  Will be "a joy forever,"
But though Devon's hill-top may be joy,
  It's "a thing of beauty" never.

T. A. S. (OH'S) LAMENT?

A VULGAR BALLAD A LA OCCIDENT.

I'M a blamed tough, ripping rider on the " bi ;"
  I'm a racer too you just can " bet your eye ;"
  I'm a terror on the " wheel,"
  A sundowner on a "steal"
For to " hook " a brand new bicycle " I'm fly."

Let me get my claws once on a handsome " bike,"
Give me twenty yards or so upon the " pike ;"
  To catch me then you'll fail
  Though you gripped the " old gent's " tail
And he rode a Hades' manufactured " trike."

149

If you own a " Rucker Tandem " or a " trike "
Or an " Expert " or some other kind of " bike,"
    Pretty " Facile " or fat " Club,"
    " Star " or any other tub,
Say your aves when you meet me on the pike.

Yes you reckon I'm a racer and all think
That I'm bound to " raise the hair" on dear old " Brink."
    Oh ! you bet he's sick and hazy
    As is every other daisy,
For of racers T. A. S.* is just " the pink."

---

* A member of the Pennsylvania Bicycle Club.

SHORT "PANTS" AND LONG LUNGS.

THERE'S a nuisance that we must abate,
  One that sorely afflicts this our town,
What it is I need only to state
  To insure its completest knock down;
And this great *crying* evil we see
  When our heart is the fullest of joy,
For that is the moment of bliss
  To the heart of the selfish small boy.

He's the nuisance that troubles this town,
  Though he's all very nice in his way,
Indeed it's a question to me
  How without him we'd live for a day:

But I tell you his worth is not quite
    Its weight in proverbial old gold,
When he takes the fell notion to make
    You, through using expletives, grow old.

Now mark! I'm in no way disposed
    To disparage our blooming young sons,
Though in matters of pleasure they purely
    Consider their sweet " Number Ones ;"
And on this very head I complain
    That the rising young nation to-day
Is addicted most strongly to some
    Most precociously smart kinds of play.

Now, for instance, when I was a boy,
    And from being so fully inclined
To indulge in all innocent larks
    Which my free roving fancy could find,
I'd play each unpatented trick
    That to youthful affection appeals,
Yet I never dared say to a " dad "
    " You're a nice looking dude upon wheels."

Now this is the nuisance I say
   That Councils must surely abate,
For, brothers, what is there at all
   In Councils, or Senate, or State,
If we cyclers can't ride at our ease
   Without hearing the pride-purging squeals
Come sailing along, from some son going wrong:
   "You're a nice looking dude upon wheels"?

———

"THE devil take the bicycle,"
   Was all the deacon said,
When bearing up against the wind
   He landed on his head;
So said his wife when putting back
   The broomstick in the shed,
While the good man wished for two stout Turks
   And a trusty feather bed.

RHYME THE LAST.

J—— —— after all the bother
  This old book has given Chris,
Will you not for once be kindly
  Every girl knows how to kiss.
Ha! you say that asking in this
  Fashion, I the boon shall miss;
Perhaps—but have you never dreamed
  That Chris would sing a song like this

www.ingramcontent.com/pod-product-compliance
Lightning Source LLC
Chambersburg PA
CBHW030556270326
41927CB00007B/950